BURN YOUR BOATS

How To Take Control Of Your Life
To Dominate The World

Lewis Wegg

Lewis Wegg

I dedicate this book to my two daughters, Martha and Maisie.

Burning One's Boat's

ALLUDES TO CERTAIN FAMOUS INCIDENTS WHERE A COMMANDER, HAVING LANDED IN A HOSTILE COUNTRY, ORDERED HIS MEN TO DESTROY THEIR SHIPS, SO THAT THEY WOULD HAVE TO CONQUER THE COUNTRY OR BE KILLED.

WHY YOU HAVE TO READ THIS BOOK

Many years ago I read something that explained how certain leaders in history would order their men after they landed on an island or any new land, to burn their boats to make sure that they had no option to return. They fought to the death and conquered. I think that's the best mind set and attitude to have in life. To make sure you are mentally prepared for anything that comes your way.

The world is a tough place. Some of the most strongest, dominant people who will mentally destroy you have the nicest smiles and appear to be the most generous. I have spent many years dealing with these kinds of people and it completely baffles me how many people out there can't even seem to put themselves first and do whatever they want without paying attention to other people's opinions.

Most people don't even know how the successful operate and have lot of hatred towards them. They say the rich need to pay more in taxes and break up the most powerful companies. You can't be rich if you think poor like the haters. Small minds have small dreams but are full of opinions which is why you need to think big. You need to learn how to dominate. Apple thought big and have dominated the handheld markets since creating the iPhone, Google with Maps, Spotify with music streaming and Uber with taxis but no one has dominated like Amazon. Jeff Bezos of Amazon, is one the smartest businessman of our time, the richest man on the planet and should be applauded on his long-term ideas. I admire him greatly. Amazon have completely taken over the entire retail industry, online web storage, video streaming with Prime and have a share of almost any industry out there. Thinking big like Amazon is a clear example that things can be done.

What is written in this book will hopefully elevate you out of the negativity you're in and boost your confidence like you have the heart of a lion. When people tell me or try to tell me about the odds, I don't care about them. I will teach you how not to either. My aim for writing this is to make you question everything you know, learn everything you can about you're doing instead of being like everyone else who just hopes for the best. Start learning like a child again. Start living to the full. This isn't a 1000-page book, it's just a collection of stories to make you think about your own life and to mould you into something far greater than you can ever be.

If you're still wanting to read on then I will give you some warnings. I am not going to sugar coat anything. Every single thing in this book is as raw as I can make it and the quotes and conversations are written as best as I can remember them. You're going to hear some stories that might not be politically correct and definitely hear some opinions which the everyday man or women may say is not fit for the mainstream media. I don't care. I had to learn at a very young age that the world is not this happy fairy-tale place. This is a dark, twisted, and fucked up world where you have to have the attitude of a lion to succeed. When I was at the lowest point in my life, which I refer to as 'Rock Bottom' I read something which has stuck to me until this very day and will do for the rest of my life.

"FIGHT IT OR ACCEPT IT."

CHAPTER ONE: THE WORLD TODAY

I think the world has changed. We use to applaud work ethic and taking risks, now we just call them stupid or having no direction. I wake up at 04:00 every day, normally in bed by 23:00. I get told how 'crazy' I am but I thought one day, how would I be able to compete with those that have already got most of their things done before the rest of the world even wakes up? When I was younger, I copied the habits of a few billionaires and stuck to them. Acting rich and thinking rich will make you rich. I tell everyone to read for an hour each morning. I tell everyone to go to bed a little earlier and be awake early enough to watch the sun rise. I also tell everyone I know to stop complaining and just get on with it. Funny how those who say they don't have enough time to go to the gym will sit there and watch Netflix all night after work without fail. I know so many people who say they can't afford to start a business but are buying new cars, new phones and even new wives. One thing I hate is people wasting time, those that just louse around until the day is up. I've worked in countless jobs where everyone is complaining they are tired on Monday. I actually said to someone once "Why don't you wake up an hour earlier and then you can be more awake when you come in?" His response was that he would then lose his 8.5 hours' worth of sleep and would need an extra coffee in the morning. Drink that extra coffee then if that's what the issue is, some days I've had 3 or 4 coffees to keep me going. You can't succeed by making excuses.

A big problem with the world today is definitely instant gratification. I know that having instant these days is normal, but success doesn't work like that. It takes 28 days to make or break a habit, almost everyone I've explained that too says it's too long to wait. Yes you can have same day shipping and digital purchases that you can use instantly, but some things do take a long time. Like relationships, friendships or being happy with yourself. Simon Sinek gave a few good speeches on this issue and I think it's a very important one. We are now entering a world of consumerism created to turn us all mediocre. Following the crowd, or as my mum calls it 'Keeping up with the Jones's' is now the new normal way to live. Binging on a weekend. Being broke a week after pay day. Of course, you will feel trying to fit in with society, but the successful are doing things differently.

Someone who knew exactly what work ethic is, was my Grandad. The last generation of hard workers. From being born into The Second World War in 1941, he saw first-hand what a catastrophe was. The Wegg family history is very short, most died young. All I know is that my Grandad's mother was from the slums of East London. After they were demolished, the government moved her to Suffolk. When he left school, they sent him to work in a factory as he couldn't read or write. From teaching himself how to do those two things which are essential for everyday life now, he managed to become an expert at maths and made himself financially independent from stocks and bonds and lived a very comfortable life. There were no electronic calculators in his days. It's hard to imagine someone today changing their lives like that because they would see something on the internet about having it instantly and lose their focus. The best things in life do take a long time. Rome wasn't built in a day.

One thing people like my Grandad hated was seeing on a daily basis was how lazy people have become with technology. Most others in my family or friends I told the same thing too normally just laughed it off, but when you sit down and think about it for a minute it does make sense. With the internet, you can search up literally anything. Wikipedia has millions of pages that are so long you can find out somebody's shoe size in less than a minute. Instead of using tech just to consume, you can use it to benefit your life. I've written nearly this whole book using my iPhone. I had to turn it on airplane mode to stop being distracted but it just proves you can get things done with a little discipline.

Now look, I know that many of you out there are stuck in a situation like I was and writing this book is my way of saying 'Hey, it's okay.' I am not the smartest person in the world. When people ask where I gained my knowledge or intelligence, I show them the books on my bookshelf. I make them watch the films that inspired me. I was like everyone else, just existing out of thin air like an NPC going to work every day and not even questioning the greater things in life.

Until it all changed in 2016.

CHAPTER TWO: LIONS WALK ALONE

A lot of people out there who don't know me personally think I was just born different or had some special trait of being successful. I would argue against that fully, because I was always just nothing special. I was born and raised in a small town in Suffolk that no one has ever heard of, I dropped out of college and was stuck working on minimum wage for many years. From going through many personal changes myself, I know that anyone out there with the right attitude to learning can be successful. A lot of you have only known me as someone who has never given up and has the attitude of a champion, but I wasn't always like that. Believe me, I wasn't. There was a time where the little boy had to grow up and be a man. Writing a book like this was something I never thought of doing. I've helped a lot of people overcome different challenges or obstacles in their lives. In some cases probably even saved lives. I don't see the point of preaching about being able to help others or bragging about how amazing my words are but if someone reading this one day gains the motivation I was given by my mentors, then please absorb everything you can. I was told to write this by many people and I think it's about time that the world was inspired once again.

My mind-set isn't for everyone. Some people find it too intimidating or my find my attitude too masculine. I'm sorry, but if that's how you think then this isn't the book for you. This is a book for those that are fed up of how life is. Are at the stage in their life where they want to be the best and are ready to change their entire existence. Some people reading this might even be in the top 1% of the richest people on the planet but have lost touch and need to come back to reality. I've been broke, homeless, lied to, backstabbed, had nothing to eat, was told at 21 I could have lymphoma in my neck and might not even make it to live another year, had sleepless nights, dealt with death, destruction, corruption, depression, addiction and have dealt with so much pain that my tear ducts don't even work anymore. I think at this point I have literally faced every challenge and set back possible, but no matter what, I will never ever give up and I hope you don't either.

I believe that to be a man, you have to transition from being a boy. The best explanation of this transition has been done by German philosopher Friedrich Nietzsche in his book *Thus Spoke Zarathustra*. Nietzshe writes about how in life you're a camel, just wondering through being told what to do. Your parents or society could be pressuring you into becoming a specific profession like how my parents always said I had to be a doctor or a lawyer otherwise I was a waste of space or could be telling you how to act or dress or what movies to watch or music to listen to. I know what it's like not being able to fit in, I look back at my younger days of being the outcast as a positive because those that fit in perfectly haven't been very successful from following the crowd. So after the 'camel' is drifting along being told what to do. The commands are coming from a dragon whose name is 'Thou Shalt.' The dragon is the saying "Thou shalt will study this." Or "Thou shalt will dress like this." Basically, the dragon is commanding and controlling the camel. This sometimes goes on for a couple of years, maybe a decade or maybe even more, I know people who are almost retirement age are listening to "Thou Shalt." Until something changes. You become a lion. You start to say no. You start thinking that you are better off alone and only you can make that change. It could be a feeling that living in your parents' home could be holding you back. It could be the relationship you're in or the friends around you that you have to say no to. What you could do is think about what could be holding you back, then say no to it all and start saying "I will." Start slaying down the dragon of "Thou Shalt" with a "I Will!" to the things you want to start doing. As much as others may love you, you have to start putting yourself first. Take the risk of burning your boats and start having the courage to take over the island. At which point you could reach your Ground Zero. Rock Bottom. Sometimes reaching rock bottom is needed. I do think that when you look at everything going wrong as a good thing, it will change your mind set instantaneously and motivate you back into the right way. Have courage though. No matter what, have the courage to continue and conquer. Sometimes your courage will hit you in the most unlikely of times.

The choice I had to make to be a man I wasn't easy. I use to be and was raised up as someone who loved security and just accepted being bossed around. Being the average person was all I was and like everyone else, I despised the successful. I thought they were the worst people on the planet and always had an anger at how they were so happy and I was not. My parents always said that rich people are evil, people who take gap years to go travelling are just throwing their lives away and people who sit all day reading books never get rich or have any direction in life. I was told during my school years that I had to become a very highly skilled worker to take care of my future wife and kids or else I'd end up at McDonald's. After finishing school with two GCSE's, dropping out of college twice and ending up working as a cook at KFC, I think it's safe to say I was the 'loser' of the family. The one they always frowned upon and looked down at. I don't care what they thought of me back then, I've let it all go and I have fantastic relationships with them now. I don't blame my mum for the ideology or advice she tried to make me follow, we are just two people on very different journeys. Looking back though, I'd say the worst point my life was when I was 19 just after getting my own place in London. I had no idea what to do or how to fix my financial mess, my personal problems or anything else. There was a point in that darkness where the changes happened. I had to slay the dragon. Everyone has to make that change and the sooner you do, the better you'll be. The best way for me to explain how you make that transition is by explaining what happened to me. How I went from the unemployed teen living with his mum, to being a mentally strong guy living in the heart of what I consider the greatest city in the world.

Essentially what triggered the whole process off was me getting fired from a factory in my home town of Ipswich, not really having anything going and explained to my mum that maybe I should go back into fast food. She made it very clear that sometimes its best you leave certain professions alone. As much as I wanted to go back to KFC, I knew I wouldn't give it my all and would simply become one those employees who aren't bad enough to fire but not good enough to promote. I was still only fresh out of a break up and that was still flipping my emotions around and I just felt like I had to get out or escape. The next day I filled my backpack of basic living essentials and got the train to London. I stayed in my Uncle's flat for a few weeks as he lived in the Netherlands but this is where the first hurdle was. I managed to get a job working in a university as a barista and I loved it, the hourly rate was much better than Ipswich and I felt like maybe this is how I want to be. I couldn't enjoy more the morning commute surrounded by city workers in suits all on their way to do big business deals and surrounded by the wealthiest on the planet. Since I worked in Moorgate, I would often sit outside on my lunch and watch them all walk on by, knowing one day I would be just like that. Instead of eating lunch outside on the street, one day I would be the one looking down at the city from the top of my own tower. It was so motivating to see. I knew I had to sort myself out in order for me to stay there. This was the choice I had to make and I chose very wisely.

The following day I was walking by a slick back man suited and booted holding a little purple book. I managed to get a glimpse of the title and it simply read Rich Dad Poor Dad. Later that night I ordered it on Amazon and within a few days of reading I was hooked. That booked changed my entire financial understanding of money and I believe everyone on the planet needs to read that book. I then had to work out my cost of living against my earnings and on paper the numbers all worked out, only just though. I would be a very tight person and couldn't enjoy myself like I use to. I couldn't ask my parents for help because I already knew what the answer was. It was the biggest change to my life so far so I made sure I was fully equipped financially and mentally. After only a couple of weeks, my uncle decided to let his flat go as he was permanently going to live in Europe, now this is where it got complicated. I had sorted the job situation out but now I had nowhere to live. As always, my family decided that it was best I came home to continue living what they said was a normal life and not to take the risk of living by myself. I was so upset that no one had any faith in choices that I had to then choose, either their predications of me failing against my own belief tat I would be okay. I didn't sleep all night and in the early hours of the morning I had made up my mind. Lewis was only going to listen to Lewis. I made it very clear to my mum I wasn't coming home, she was very scared but if I tried to explain to her how much faith in myself I had at the time, she wouldn't of listened anyway. It's like we were speaking different languages. By the end of that week I had my own place and there I was, a man. Or so I thought.

Being 19 and now alone in a city of almost 10 million trying to survive on my own two feet with no help at all was not easy. I couldn't go out or spend as I wanted, I was hours away from my family and friends and I had no idea how to even work out what the bus routes were or how to even use the tube. I had a small lump of cash and barely just paid the deposit and fees on a little studio flat. Now I was completely broke. My dad called me saying that if I stayed in London, I would be making the worst decision of my life but you know what, it was one of my best. I was free. I was completely free from anyone and anything. I had burned my boats. There was no turning back now. It was Lewis' time to shine. The next couple of months were some of the hardest I have ever gone through but going through that storm was needed. It's a bit like when someone you have trusted over the years has stabbed you in the back, you needed closure on that friendship. I had hope in myself. I believed in myself for the first time and I still do.

The easiest way to summarise that point of my life is to realise that's where it all began. Starting your own journey by yourself and go out alone. I wasn't raised up to be like how I am now, I learnt all of that myself. The people around me never told me to read books, dream big or aspire to be the richest man in the world. They said to get a very secure job and live a quiet peaceful life. Don't be loud or draw attention to yourself, don't be tough on people and to help those who are in need, even if they are bad or abusive to you. Doesn't exactly fit my personality now, does it? Maybe other people in a similar situation to how I was just need to get out from where they are mentally or physically and start from scratch. You may not have the safety net of your parents but to develop into a man and to learn how to stand on your own two feet is absolutely necessary if you want to be successful.

Leave the safety net of your parents if you're still living with them, go and travel if you haven't seen the world, go and live in any city or country you want to and live how you want to live. You have no idea how many people I know that have fantastic business ideas that will be great successes but won't go ahead with them because they are worried it won't work. They say they earn more money doing their day job, it's too risky to create a business when most of them fail or the best excuse I hear is that they don't have the time or are too old. Ray Croc didn't start McDonald's until he was 52, Colonel Sanders created KFC at 62 and Donald Trump became President of The United States at 70.

I was listening to a speech by the richest man in the world, Jeff Bezos of Amazon, where he said that when he first thought of creating Amazon and quitting his job on Wall Street, he was worried it wouldn't all work out and he would lose the life savings of his parents who had invested in his idea. One night he thought about when he was 80. Being an old man looking back on his life, he knew he wouldn't look back and regret ever trying and will be glad to of had the courage to take that risk and give it his best shot. It's hard to imagine a world without Amazon but the whole idea was just down to one decision. It's a very good outlook on life to have which I follow too.

So, ask yourself when you're 80 and looking back at today. What will you be glad you had the courage to do?

CHAPTER THREE: ROCK BOTTOM

"Is this a blip, or this a catastrophe? Now a catastrophe is a tsunami, an earthquake or a war. And a blip is everything else." – Donald Trump

One of my favourite movies of all time is The Grey. The reason I absolutely love this film is because it gives a clear philosophical message. The Will to Live. The film is based on a group of survivors trying to survive after their plane crashes in a remote part of the Alaskan wilderness. At the beginning of the film, Liam Neeson's character Ottway tries to commit suicide. He has lost his wife and has made the decision he has nothing to live for. After the plane crashes he realises that he wasn't just going to survive a catastrophe like that just to give up. Throughout the film, many of those who survived just accept their fate and decide there isn't any point of even trying but Ottway decides differently. Before the film was released, the director Joe Carnahan decided to pull some of the final scenes of Liam Neeson fighting the wolves and I think it has been one of the best creative decisions about the film. Lots of people who have seen it have all said they wish they could have seen the fight but I think it's perfect as it is. It's not about fighting the wolves, it's about having the will to fight. To fight to the death. Which is why I named this book Burn Your Boats. I think that's probably where the saying 'Fight It or Accept It' came from too. Many films have touched me in a very certain way that completely changed my life and this was one of them. An important part of becoming a man is the mind-set.

In the previous chapter I talked out how I wasn't just born the way I am, it took a long time and it took many people to change the course of my life to push me in the right mind-set and mould me into the right shape for dominance. The best mentors I've ever had in my life aren't the ones who only told me what actions to take or what decisions to make, they gave me the philosophies, the wisdom, the mind-set and the courage to deal with everything that hit my way. I can still hear their voices in my head screaming and shouting at me like it was yesterday. Many years ago, I was in a very desperate position. I had very serious thoughts about ending it all, a very dark time in my life. I never really talk about because it sometimes embarrasses me that I somehow got that bad but someone helped me get through it and forced me to man up and change how I saw everything.

One of the wisest people I have ever met was my sensei, Denise. After getting my studio flat set up when I was a teenager alone in London, I use to walk past this dojo every morning I went to work and every evening I came home. Sometimes it was very early hours in the morning I would return home to make ends meet but this little dojo always caught my eye. Since I was a young boy, I have always been a big fan of Batman. Being a skinny little boy meant I was also big fan of martial arts and fighting, as I had no idea how to defend myself against anyone. I hadn't ever won a fight and every time I took a punch, it hurt a lot. One day I was in a terrible state of mind, I just got let go of another job. I was really contemplating even staying in London. I had made up my mind the next day that I was going to move back to my home town and start my life again so as a kind gesture to myself, I flipped a coin and said if heads won then I wold walk in. Heads won and the next day I entered the dojo to see what it's all about. For anyone wandering whether to do things alone, I would say go for it. Go visit that place by yourself, go venture out on your own and if your friends or people around you aren't interested, there is no better company than yourself. I will always be grateful that convincing myself to walk in would introduce me to someone who I will never forget. She was a one of a kind, had very old-fashioned methods of training which looking back were very brutal, but absolutely necessary. I have never met anyone with the wisdom and attitude to life that she had. Denise was not an easy-going person. The best way I could describe her is the same as the music teacher Fletcher from the film Whiplash. She would scream in your face and would make sure that you left every session so worn out that you would wish you never went back. After filling out some paperwork she stopped me signing the bottom and said 'I have a few rules which you need to know, so if you don't like them, you can leave right now and there will be no harsh feelings."

Rule 1: Your ego is left at the door.
Rule 2: The session ends when I say I so, not the clock.
Rule 3: Treat everyone the same with the highest respect.

I was a broken skinny kid who walked in and by time she was finished with me, I wasn't just a man, I was a machine. What started off as a weekly martial arts class turned into her mentoring me on basically everything going on in my life. She taught me in a very particular style that you don't get in a normal school, it's a little old fashioned and definitely not politically correct. I remember one time I was doing high kicks and she walked over to me and quietly whispered in my ear in a sweet soft tone "Are you alright Lewis? Is your leg broken?" I then politely explained to her that my leg was fine and I was simply just tired from a long day in the office. Before I could even finish my sentence she screamed at the top of her lungs, so loud that you could hear a mile away, "THEN LEFT UP YOUR LEG BOY!" With both of her hands she grabbed my foot and yanked my leg up so high I felt like it was going to snap off. Having someone push you beyond anything you thought was imaginable is what you need. You don't need polite people telling you how amazing you are, you need someone to eat you up and spit you out. After a couple of weeks from trying to keep up with her training and failing beyond belief with it all, I essentially just gave up.

One lesson I was struggling really bad. It was just after a 12-hour shift from work and I was knackered, I was struggling to stay awake let alone be able to push myself to the extend she wanted. She made me punch the boxing bag as fast as I could to make it swing against the wall and stay touching the wall for 2 minutes. After the two minutes was up, she asked for another two and another until I ended up just staring at the clock hoping for the lesson to be over. I had just lost my job, ran out of money and felt like I was a complete waste of space. After several attempts at the bag I just walked over to the corner of the dojo and collapsed into the corner. She watched me on the other side of the room and just gave me a very blank look. A few minutes later, she walked over and sat next to me. I felt like balling my eyes out. I didn't know how to handle stress, I had no one to turn to and above all I wasn't even strong enough to finish a fucking martial arts lesson. But what she said to me was something that opened my eyes and changed my perspective on it all. She asked what was wrong and after explaining my awful day she made me attempt the bag again to clear my mind. It didn't work and I was back slumped over in the corner again. After shaking her head a few times, she leant over with her hands over her knees and said "You have to be tougher than this Lewis. If you can't defend yourself here then what are you going to do when you're out in the real world? Your struggles are in your mind, they aren't real. It doesn't matter what your family think of you. It doesn't matter what you've done in the past. I don't care your money issues, your loneliness, it doesn't matter."

Panting away trying to get my breath back, I said. "I've tried my best Denise. I can't to it."

"I know you can. Full stop." She said very firmly.

I looked up into her eyes and just shook my head. She then leant in very slowly and said to me in one of the most serious tones I've ever heard in her voice. "There are people training in caves, with nothing to eat and they are 10 times the strength of you." I paused for a second and she walked away. What a statement it was. There are people out there who can't walk, get terminal illnesses and have tragedies a lot worse than what I was going through. Donald Trump explained it in a similar way. "Is this a blip, or is this a catastrophe? Now a catastrophe is an earthquake, a tsunami or a war. And a blip is everything else." Advice I will follow every single day. Makes you realise that all of the difficulty you're going through is just a blip, follow that advice and it will instantaneously change your perspective on things.

A little while after I left London I went back to the dojo to find it replaced by a new business and completely lost touch with her. So if you ever end up reading this Denise, you have no idea how much you have helped me. The wisdom you have taught me. Find yourself mentors who will elevate you, intimidate you to push yourself and make sure that every single day you are alive, you are making yourself better. That's what Denise did for me and I hope you can find someone to do the same with you. The attitude she taught me to have was one of a warrior, a champion, a lion. "Kill me or I'll starve." That's been my attitude since I was 19 years old and I will stick with that attitude until the day I die.

CHAPTER FOUR:
THE MINDSET

C oming out of 'Rock Bottom' was not easy at all. It won't be easy for you either. The changes I had to go through were many sleepless nights, lots of pain and stress and at times really made me question it all. Toughen up as much as you can and be prepared for life. Unfortunately, there will be some consequences for every action you take.

The movie *Batman v Superman: Dawn of Justice* is my favourite movie of all time. There is a scene where Clark Kent is in a troubled state and wanders up some mountains to where he sees a vision of his dad telling an old story. Basically, as Superman, he realised he can't save everyone and by saving one person, he then has to let somebody else go unsaved. The story his dad explains is about how when his dad was young, there was bad rain one year which caused a flood nearly destroying the farm. They worked all night building a blockade to stop the water, which was successful, but then caused the neighbours farm to flood killing their horses. His dad said he use to hear them wailing in his sleep. Clark then asks if his nightmares ever stopped, his dad replied "Yeah, when I met your mother. She gave me faith that there is good in this world." One of the most powerful scenes I have ever watched in a film and it tears me up every time I watch it. No matter what action you take, there will be a consequence and you need to find a way of dealing with it internally.

Staying focused is a big part of success and a major part of dominating. I'd say 99% of the world can't focus for more than a few minutes without being distracted. Humans really are no better than goldfish. When I'm at the gym, I use an iPod and leave my phone in the car. Means I have no choice but to focus on working out and can't just keep getting distracted by notifications. I started making the disconnect a few years ago by actually turning notifications off on my phone, then deleting anything that was using up my time. You might end up missing what your friends had for dinner or how great their holiday was, but what you create with your own time will be far greater. Invest your time in yourself. It's not easy, but it is simple. Write a list of everything you want to change about yourself and start with one change per month. Listed below are some habits, books to read and movies to watch that have turned me into the man I am and will change your life too. I wrote this book to make you think and to correct the course you are on. Let this day be the dawn of your new life.

An easy habit to begin with is waking up an hour earlier. Grab a cup of coffee, read the morning news and then start using your free time much better. I normally workout, read or listen to some motivating things. Another easy habit to form is going to the gym. After you come home, allocate one day a week where you go to the gym. The hardest part is getting there and the hardest day will always be your first. After you have gone for a month or so, start going twice a week and keep building that habit to make it a fundamental thing like brushing your teeth or showering.

The book you need to read today is *Rich Dad Poor Dad* by Robert Kiyosaki. It will change how you view money and really change the way you think about what wealth is. I read this book when I was 20 and have read it probably over 100 times. After that you should read, *The Richest Man in Babylon*. Another one of my favourite books. Rules of money from thousands of years ago which will work thousands of years in the future. I have a massive interest in ancient civilisations so reading about a finance book on them was icing on the cake.

The film you need to see tonight will be The Grey featuring Liam Neeson. It will show you what 'Fight it or accept it' is. The will to live. I like watching films that are very emotional, have a big meaning to the story and that have characters I can relate to. Another great film I love is 12 Years a Slave. I have read the book it was based on and I think the film shows perfectly the emotions of the slaves going through what they went through. One of the greatest people I have ever listened to is T.D Jakes. He said many years ago in a speech that you need to have courage. "Do you have the courage, to stand there while the storm keep raging?" Very powerful. He also said "After all my ancestors have been through and all that my parents have been through. I didn't go through all of that just to fit in with normalcy." I had to listen to it about 10 times on repeat because after watching a film like 12 Years a Slave, it really makes you think what people in this world have gone through so we can live a normal life. His ancestors were slaves for decades. My ancestors sat in a ditch for 4 years in World War One and gave their lives making sure that the future generations could live a life of freedom. Really powerful speech he said. Opened my eyes fully.

Find yourself some mentors and follow some of their rules and ideology. One of the biggest mentors in my life is Donald Trump. I unfortunately have never had the chance to meet him but there have been many bad or difficult times where I've heard his voice echo in my head. I don't care about politics and don't care whether you like him or not. A very high-performance person. Listen to someone who really motivates you like The President does for me. Trump was a smart guy, and I listened very carefully to everything he said about business and life.

FINAL THOUGHTS

Hopefully after reading this book, you will feel better about yourself and start taking risks. Start living a life of adventure and not doing what others have pressured you into. Slay the dragon of 'Thou Shalt' and put yourself first. Don't ever feel bad about putting yourself first, I do it every day and have great success by doing it. You have to be tough. Mentally and physically. Start a routine of going to the gym, or purchase some equipment to use at home, give yourself some discipline in your life. Make sure that your defence is the highest it can be. Protect yourself from all angles of other people's deception. They will do everything they can to bring you down. Another thing you must have is focus and patience. Rome wasn't built in a day and changing your habits will take lots of failures to finally succeed. Don't be scared of the failing part, be excited for the success of it. Sailing against the wind will not be easy. Don't let anyone divert your course or influence you in a negative way to stop you. If at any point you lose your focus, read this book again and get back to working on whatever it was you were. Find someone who motivates you and find out what they do on a daily basis, listen to them every day and read any books they have written.

Sometimes forcing yourself into a situation will leave you with no choice but to go ahead with it. As Bezos said, when you're 80 and looking back on your life, you won't regret the trying and failing but you will always regret not going ahead with it because you'll never know how successful you could have been. I never thought of writing a book and having the courage to do so forced me to write it and I would like to say thank you for reading it. This may not be the best book ever written but it is my beginning. Put yourself on the island and burn your boats.

There is no turning back now.

Lewis Wegg

ABOUT THE AUTHOR

Lewis Wegg

Lewis Wegg is a British author from Ipswich, England.

www.ingramcontent.com/pod-product-compliance
Lightning Source LLC
Chambersburg PA
CBHW030600220526

45463CB00007B/3128